Rihanna

By Mary Kate Frank

 Gareth Stevens
Publishing

Please visit our web site at www.garethstevens.com.
For a free catalog describing Gareth Stevens Publishing's list of high-quality books,
call 1-800-542-2595 (USA) or 1-800-387-3178 (Canada).
Gareth Stevens Publishing's fax: 1-877-542-2596

Library of Congress Cataloging-in-Publication Data
Frank, Mary Kate.
   Rihanna / by Mary Kate Frank.
      p. cm. — (Today's superstars)
   Includes bibliographical references and index.
   ISBN-10: 1-4339-2379-3   ISBN-13: 978-1-4339-2379-1 (lib. bdg.)
   ISBN-10: 1-4339-2375-0   ISBN-13: 978-1-4339-2375-3 (soft cover)
   1. Rihanna, 1988– —Juvenile literature. 2. Singers—Biography—Juvenile literature. I. Title.
ML3930.R44F73 2010
782.42164092—dc22 [B]   2009007171

This edition first published in 2010 by
Gareth Stevens Publishing
A Weekly Reader® Company
1 Reader's Digest Road
Pleasantville, NY 10570-7000 USA

Copyright © 2010 by Gareth Stevens, Inc.

Executive Managing Editor: Lisa M. Herrington
Senior Designer: Keith Plechaty

Art Direction and Page Production: The Design Lab

Photo Credits: cover, title page Wolfgang Rattay/Reuters/Corbis; p. 4 Scott Gries/Getty Images
for Universal Music; p. 6 Gary Hershorn/Reuters/Corbis; p. 7 Brian Zak/Sipa Press /rihanna_
bz.05/0806201755 (Sipa via AP Images); p. 8, 46 Atlantide Phototravel/Corbis; p. 9 AP Photo/Jennifer
Graylock; p. 10 Douglas Pearson/Corbis; p. 12 Andre Gallant/Getty Images; p. 13 Fridmar Damm/zefa/
Corbis; p. 14 Lawrence Manning/Corbis; p. 15 Lynn Goldsmith/Corbis; p. 16, 46 top AP Photo/Kristie
Bull/Graylock.com; p. 18 Mikhael Subotzky/Corbis; p. 19 Rob Rich/Everett Collection; p. 20 AP Photo/
Kristie Bull/Graylock.com; p. 21 Brad Barket/Getty Images; p. 22 AP Photo/Tammie Arroyo; p. 24 AP
Photo/Kathy Willens; p. 25 AP Photo/Jennifer Graylock; p. 26, 41 AP Photo/Chris Carlson; p. 27 top
AP Photo/Kirsty Wigglesworth; p. 27 bottom Kevin Winter/Getty Images; p. 28 Paul McConnell/Getty
Images; p. 30 AP Photo/Mark J. Terrill; p. 31 Amanda Edwards/Getty Images; p. 32 Heidi Gutman/
NBC NewsWire via AP Images; p. 33 top Andrew Gombert/epa/Corbis; p. 33 bottom AP Photo/Jeff
Christensen; p. 34 AP Photo/CP, Aaron Harris; p. 36 AP Photo/Evan Agostini; p. 38 Shutterstock/glo; p. 39
AP Photo/Evan Agostini; p. 44 Shutterstock/Yevgeny Gultaev; p. 48 Maggie McGill

Printed in the United States of America

1 2 3 4 5 6 7 8 9 14 13 12 11 10 09

Contents

Words in the glossary appear in **bold** type the first time they are used in the text.

Rihanna was born and raised on the island of Barbados.

Chapter 1

Homecoming

Thousands of people crowded around a stage in Bridgetown, Barbados, on February 21, 2008. They were welcoming home a local girl turned star. Barbados-born singer Rihanna had recently won music's highest honor, a Grammy Award. She had also turned 20 on February 20.

Prime Minister David Thompson, the Caribbean nation's leader, had a special birthday gift. He named Rihanna an honorary cultural **ambassador** for Barbados. That means she will help represent Barbados wherever she goes.

People who are from Barbados are called Bajans. "I am so grateful," she told the crowd, "and I have never been more proud to be Bajan."

Pop Princess

Rihanna's first record, 2005's *Music of the Sun*, sold more than 2 million copies worldwide. Her next two, *A Girl Like Me* and *Good Girl Gone Bad*, were bigger hits. Those records produced four number-one singles and a dozen top 40 singles.

Her most famous song is "Umbrella." The song earned Rihanna her first Grammy Award, for Best Rap/Sung **Collaboration**. She shared the award with her partner on the song, rapper Jay-Z.

TRUE OR FALSE?

Rihanna is the first Bajan artist to win a Grammy Award.

For answers, see page 46.

Teaming Up

Many of the biggest talents in music have worked with Rihanna. Singer Ne-Yo wrote Rihanna's hit "Unfaithful." Pop star Justin Timberlake wrote the song "Rehab" for her. She sang on rapper T.I.'s single "Live Your Life." It went to number one on the *Billboard* charts. She also sang with the pop rock band Maroon 5 on her song "If I Never See Your Face Again."

◀ Ne-Yo appears with Rihanna at the 2006 MTV Video Music Awards.

Fashion Forward

Rihanna is famous for more than her music. Her unique style has landed her on magazine covers worldwide. And her face is known to people everywhere. She isn't afraid to take chances when it comes to fashion.

"I love to play to both sides of my personality — the girlie and the tough," she told *InStyle* magazine. "That's what makes my style different."

▶ Rihanna has a unique fashion sense. It makes her a favorite subject for photographers.

Leaving Home

At the start of 2003, Rihanna was just a normal teenager growing up in St. Michael, Barbados. She enjoyed singing and pretending she was onstage. "I would hold a broom like a mic stand," she told *Rolling Stone* magazine. "My neighbors would complain—they always knew when I was home."

In December 2003, Rihanna met a music **producer** who was vacationing in Barbados. The producer wanted to make 15-year-old Rihanna a star. In order to pursue her dream, Rihanna had to move to the United States.

TRUE OR FALSE?

Rihanna's favorite meal is a salad.

▼ Barbados's beautiful beaches make it a top destination for vacationers.

8

All About Rihanna

Name: Robyn Rihanna Fenty

Birth Date: February 20, 1988

Birthplace: St. Michael, Barbados

Height: 5 feet 9 inches (175 centimeters)

Hair: Black

Eyes: Green

Current Home: Los Angeles, California

Family: Parents Ronald and Monica; two younger brothers, Rorrey and Rajad

Believing in Herself

The sacrifices that Rihanna made for her career have paid off. Today, she has the best of both worlds. She lives in Los Angeles, California. And she visits Barbados when she isn't busy working.

Rihanna credits her belief in herself for her amazing success. "When I was young, I would watch award shows and be like, 'I want to do that one day,'" she told *Seventeen* magazine. "I would practice speeches and silly stuff ... I just knew that this is what I wanted—and somehow I just knew it would happen."

Fact File

One of the first books Rihanna read after moving to the United States was *Adventures of Huckleberry Finn* by Mark Twain.

"[In Barbados] I would climb trees, steal mangoes, catch birds—silly things THAT WERE FUN TO US AT THE TIME."

—Rihanna

Bridgetown is the capital city of Barbados.

Chapter 2
Island Girl

Robyn Rihanna Fenty was born on February 20, 1988, in St. Michael, on the Caribbean island of Barbados. Her father, Ronald, was a warehouse supervisor at a garment factory. Her mother, Monica, was an accountant. Today, Monica owns a clothing shop.

Rihanna is close with her two younger brothers, Rorrey and Rajad. Growing up, she sometimes even borrowed her brothers' clothes!

"I wore my brothers' clothes, dresses with sneakers, or no shoes at all," she told *InStyle*. They all enjoyed life on Barbados. "I would climb trees, steal mangoes, catch birds—silly things that were fun to us at the time."

Family Ties

Rihanna's childhood wasn't easy. Her father had a drug problem. This led her parents to separate. They divorced when she was 14.

Rihanna and her brothers stopped visiting their father because of his **addiction**. "My mom would take us to see him, and he would be in the worst condition," Rihanna remembers. "She stopped taking us because she didn't want us to see him like that." Today, Rihanna's dad is drug-free, and they are close once again.

◀ Like these Bajan children, Rihanna grew up with big dreams for her future.

Life in Barbados

What was Rihanna's favorite part of growing up on Barbados? The warm weather! The average temperature there is 70 to 75 degrees Fahrenheit (21 to 24 degrees Celsius).

Rihanna enjoys talking about life in Barbados. She has found out that a lot of people don't know much about her home country. "Someone asked me if we have indoor toilets," she told *Allure*. "I can't get upset. They just don't know." (For the record, the answer to that question is yes!)

Finding Music

Rihanna's mom is black. Her dad is of mixed race. At school, girls bullied Rihanna because of her light skin. "I didn't understand," she recalls. "I just knew I saw people of all different shades, and I was light."

Music was Rihanna's comfort and escape. She often shut herself in her room and pretended she was a famous singer. "I'd sing in the mirror with a brush," she told *Seventeen* magazine.

Fact File
Even though she grew up on an island, Rihanna has said that she is afraid of the ocean.

▲ Singing groups like this one inspired Rihanna to form a group with her friends.

Fact File

Rihanna won her high school talent show by singing Mariah Carey's song "Hero."

A Big Break

In high school, Rihanna formed a singing group with two girlfriends. But they never decided on a name. Then in December 2003, Rihanna, 15, met music producer Evan Rogers while he was vacationing in Barbados. Her group **auditioned** for him.

The young singer made a big impression on the producer. "The minute Rihanna walked into the room, it was like the other two girls didn't exist," Rogers later told *Entertainment Weekly*.

On Her Way

Before she could get a record deal, Rihanna had to make a **demo**. A demo is a recording of a few songs that can be sent out to record labels. Over the next year, she worked on her demo, traveling between Barbados and Rogers's home in Stamford, Connecticut.

It became hard for Rihanna to juggle her music with school in Barbados. Rogers invited Rihanna to move in with him and his wife in Connecticut. The island girl was on her way to the United States.

Fact File

Evan Rogers has written songs for Christina Aguilera and Kelly Clarkson.

Reggae Rules!

Reggae is a type of music that developed on the Caribbean island of Jamaica in the late 1960s. Reggae blends many styles such as rhythm and blues and jazz. The song lyrics often concern social or political issues. Rihanna's sound is heavily influenced by reggae. At her concerts, she often sings songs made famous by reggae artist Bob Marley.

▶ **Bob Marley was the most famous reggae performer.**

"When I left Barbados, I DIDN'T LOOK BACK."
—Rihanna

Rihanna followed her dreams and quickly became a superstar.

Chapter 3

In America

After she moved to producer Evan Rogers's home in Stamford, Connecticut, life was busy for Rihanna. She continued working on her music and took dance lessons. She also studied 15 hours a week with a tutor to finish high school.

"When I left Barbados, I didn't look back," Rihanna later said. "I wanted to do what I had to do [to succeed], even if it meant moving to America."

In early 2005, her four-song demo was ready to be sent to record labels. Rogers thought his new artist—still known as Robyn back then—needed a flashier stage name. She decided to go by her middle name, Rihanna.

Jay-Z Calling

Only 48 hours after Rihanna's music went out to record executives, she got an important phone call. Rapper Jay-Z, the head of Def Jam Recordings, wanted to meet with her in New York City. Rihanna fell to the floor in disbelief after hearing the news.

Before auditioning for Jay-Z, Rihanna was nervous. She didn't need to be so worried. Just hours after her audition, she had a record contract with Def Jam.

Fact File

Jay-Z has said it took him two minutes to see that Rihanna was a star.

Jay-Z's World

Jay-Z—real name Shawn Carter—is a superstar himself. He has sold more than 30 million records since his 1996 **debut**, *Reasonable Doubt*. As president of Def Jam, Jay-Z signed Rihanna and singer Ne-Yo, among other artists. In 2007, he stepped down as the label's head to focus on recording his own music. In April 2008, Jay-Z married his longtime girlfriend, singer Beyoncé Knowles.

◀ Jay-Z is one of rap music's most successful performers and producers.

Into the Studio

Rihanna called her first album *Music of the Sun*. The name was a **tribute** to the sunny island of Barbados. "The word 'sun' represents my culture where I'm from, the Caribbean," Rihanna explained to KidzWorld.com.

With the help of her producers, Rihanna cowrote four of the album's 12 songs. Most of *Music of the Sun* is fast-paced dance music. Rihanna especially liked the album's two **ballads**, "Now I Know" and "The Last Time."

▶ Jay-Z (left) has played a major role in Rihanna's career.

TRUE OR FALSE?

Early in her career, Rihanna was the opening act on a tour with Beyoncé.

Pon de … Huh?

What does "pon de replay" actually mean? Rihanna says the phrase is often heard in the dance clubs of Barbados. On the island, *pon* is a way of saying "on," and *de* means "the." "It's just basically telling the DJ to put my song on the replay," Rihanna explained. In other words, play it again!

◀ **Rihanna loves to share her music with fans.**

The Big Day

"Pon de Replay" was Rihanna's first single. It hit the airwaves on March 17, 2005. The first time she heard the song on the radio, she started screaming.

On August 30, 2005, *Music of the Sun* was released. It sold 69,000 copies its first week, landing at number 10 on the Billboard 200 chart. The record got mixed reviews from the critics. But listeners loved it. Soon, Rihanna had a following.

TRUE OR FALSE?

Rihanna's first single, "Pon de Replay," reached number one on the Billboard Hot 100.

Going Gold

In November 2006, *Music of the Sun* was certified gold. That means it had sold 500,000 copies in the United States. The album later reached platinum status by selling 1 million copies.

Rihanna had been practicing signing her autograph for years. With all her new fans, however, she had to learn to sign her name faster. "People told me [my autograph] was a bit too proper for when you're in a hurry and you've got 100 people poking things at you," she told *People*. For Rihanna, there was no time to waste. She was already thinking about her next album.

Fact File

Rihanna loves to play pranks on her friends. She once squeezed lemon juice into a sleeping friend's mouth!

▼ **Rihanna signs album inserts for eager fans.**

Rihanna wasted no time getting back into the studio to record her second album.

Chapter 4
A Girl Like Me

Most artists wait a year or more between record releases. But not Rihanna. Less than eight months after *Music of the Sun* debuted, Rihanna's second album was ready to go.

"I just love making music and the label loves to put me in the studio, so that always works great together," she explained to *Jet* magazine. "We never wanted to take a break."

Rihanna said that her second album, *A Girl Like Me*, was about not only her own experiences but also those of all girls her age. The album featured music of many styles, including reggae, disco, and rock and roll.

"Give That to Me!"

In March 2006, Rihanna released her new single, "S.O.S. (Rescue Me)." She says "S.O.S." was originally offered to singer Christina Milian. But Milian did not want to record it. "A lot of songs people pass on, and then I hear them, and I'm like, 'What were they thinking? Give that to me!' " Rihanna told *Allure* magazine.

Recording "S.O.S." proved to be a good move for Rihanna. The song was her first number-one single. It reached number one in the United States and Australia. It also hit the top five in Canada, Germany, and the United Kingdom.

◀ Rihanna performed the National Anthem at New York's Yankee Stadium in 2006.

Acting? Bring It On!

In August 2006, Rihanna made her movie debut in *Bring It On: All or Nothing*. The movie is about two competing high school cheerleading squads. The movie starred Solange Knowles Smith (Beyoncé's sister). Rihanna played herself, hosting the big cheerleading competition at the end of the film. She enjoyed the experience and would like to do more acting in the future.

▶ Rihanna enjoyed her first movie role and hopes to do more acting.

Top of the Charts

In April 2006, Rihanna's second album, *A Girl Like Me*, hit stores. The album featured 13 songs along with three bonus tracks. Many of her new songs concerned love and relationships.

A Girl Like Me sold more than 115,000 copies during its first week. Then it kept on selling. It eventually reached platinum status. The album also hit the top 10 in at least eight other countries.

Fact File

The backup music on "S.O.S." is sampled from the 1981 hit song "Tainted Love" by Soft Cell.

Billboard Champ

In addition to "S.O.S.," *A Girl Like Me* had other hit singles. "Unfaithful" and "Break It Off" both reached the top 10 in the United States.

In December 2006, Rihanna attended the Billboard Music Awards. These awards are based on record sales and radio airplay. She took home three awards, including Female Artist of the Year. "I really can't feel my legs," she told *People* magazine after her win. "This is phenomenal."

Fact File

Rihanna has a white toy poodle named DJ.

◀ Rihanna poses with one of her Billboard Music Awards in 2006.

Another Beyoncé?

When asked about her musical idols, Rihanna often mentions pop star and actress Beyoncé. Critics often compared the two stars. Some even called Rihanna the Bajan Beyoncé.

"I'm flattered when people compare me to her," Rihanna told *Jet* magazine. "But it does get a little upsetting when people say I copy her." Rihanna didn't have to worry. Her next album would leave no doubt that she was a true original.

▲ Rihanna is upset by comments that she copies Beyoncé Knowles (above).

Hometown Pride—and Criticism

In Barbados, most people were proud of Rihanna. Some Bajans criticized the young star, however. They said she dressed inappropriately. Local writers also complained that she did not give enough interviews to the media in Barbados. Rihanna doesn't let the criticism get to her. Whether people love or hate her, she says she still does what she wants to do.

▶ Some critics complain that Rihanna dresses inappropriately.

—Rihanna, talking about *Good Girl Gone Bad*

With her third album, Rihanna began to change her image. Soon, these long locks would be gone.

Chapter 5
Breaking Through

In early 2007, as Rihanna prepared to record her third album, she felt ready for a change. She wanted to separate herself from other young female singers. She decided that her new album would have a different sound.

"I just told [my record label], 'On this album, I don't want it to be only girly, only fun,' " Rihanna recalled. " 'I want it to be edgy. I want it to be one of those records that you never forget.' I knew exactly who I was, what I wanted to do, what I wanted to sound like, look like, dress like, act like, and that's exactly what I did."

Rihanna had definitely come a long way. She decided to call the album *Good Girl Gone Bad*.

Fact File

Rihanna designed
her own line of
five umbrellas for
a British company
called Totes.

A New Number One

In March 2007, Rihanna released her new single, "Umbrella." The song's catchy **chorus** quickly became famous. "You can stand under my umbrella ella ella," Rihanna sang.

"When she recorded the 'ellas,' you knew … your life was about to change if you had anything to do with that record," Christopher "Tricky" Stewart, who produced "Umbrella," told MTV. "Umbrella" went to number one and stayed there for seven straight weeks.

Good Girl Takes Off

On June 5, 2007, Rihanna released her new album *Good Girl Gone Bad.* Artists such as Timbaland and will.i.am worked on the project. In addition to "Umbrella," the album produced the hit singles "Hate That I Love You" and "Don't Stop the Music." The album was a huge success. By early 2009, it had sold more than 7 million copies worldwide.

A New Look

Before Rihanna was photographed for her new album cover, she asked a hairstylist to cut her long hair to her chin. She also dyed her hair from brown to black. "The [record] label didn't want me to do this look," Rihanna told *Allure.* "But cutting my hair, it made me stand out as an artist. I don't care who likes it—this is me."

◀ Rihanna's short haircut made headlines in 2007.

▲ Rihanna performs on the *Today* show in 2007.

Fact File

Rihanna loves to shop and owns more than 100 pairs of shoes.

On the Road

In the fall of 2007, Rihanna began her first headlining tour. The shows began in Vancouver, Canada, then moved to the United States. In November, her tour traveled to Europe and continued on to Africa, Asia, and Australia. By early 2009, Rihanna had played about 80 dates.

Singer Chris Brown was also part of the tour. Brown and Rihanna have both achieved incredible success at a young age. The two soon started dating.

Taking Home Trophies

In September 2007, Rihanna won two MTV Video Music Awards, including Video of the Year for "Umbrella." Then on February 10, 2008, she and Jay-Z won a Grammy for Best Rap/Sung Collaboration for "Umbrella." "Dad, I know I promised you I'd give you my first Grammy, but we're going to have to fight for this one!" Rihanna said from the stage.

▲ Rihanna won her first Grammy Award in 2008.

Everyone Under the Umbrella

"Umbrella" was such a popular song that other artists wanted to sing it, too. Many people sang **cover versions** of the hit song. Pop singer Mandy Moore performed "Umbrella" accompanied only by her guitar. Alternative bands such as My Chemical Romance and Linkin Park covered the song in concerts. Country singers Carrie Underwood and Keith Urban turned "Umbrella" into a **duet** when they sang it live in concert.

◀ Carrie Underwood is one of the many artists who have performed the song "Umbrella."

"I'm all about my career right now because THERE'S SO MUCH FOR ME TO DO."

—Rihanna

Rihanna appreciates all that her fans have done to keep her on top of the charts.

Chapter 6
Take a Bow

Rihanna's third record, *Good Girl Gone Bad*, did so well that she decided to release it again. Rereleasing hit records has become a common practice in the music industry. (Usher, Jessica Simpson, and 50 Cent are among the stars who have rereleased their records.) Rereleases usually contain new songs, new album artwork, and other bonuses, making them attractive to fans.

On June 17, 2008, *Good Girl Gone Bad: Reloaded* hit stores. In addition to the original music, the record included three brand-new songs. It also had a DVD of behind-the-scenes footage from Rihanna's tour. Two of the new songs—"Take a Bow" and "Disturbia"—went to number one on the Billboard chart.

▲ Rihanna poses with a group of her fans at New York City's Empire State Building in 2008.

TRUE OR FALSE?

Rihanna has a tattoo of the symbol for her astrological sign, which is Pisces.

Helping Young Fans

Rihanna has a soft spot for kids. When thinking of ways to put her fame to good use, she decided to help children. Rihanna started the Believe Foundation. This organization provides food, medicine, schooling, and other necessities to needy children all over the world.

In the spring of 2008, the Believe Foundation hosted concerts to benefit local charities in Chicago, New York, and San Francisco. In each of the cities, Rihanna performed a show for kids.

Sweet Charity

In December 2008, Rihanna found a way to benefit two of her biggest interests: fashion and children. She modeled in a series of ads for Gucci, a world-famous fashion label. The products in the ads were specially made to benefit the United Nations Children's Fund (UNICEF). Gucci donated 25 percent of its sales to UNICEF programs that help needy kids in Africa.

Fact File

In 2008, Rihanna toured with rapper Kanye West as part of his "Glow in the Dark" tour.

On January 20, 2009, Rihanna headlined a charity ball for President Barack Obama's **inauguration**. The Recording Industry Association of America (RIAA) hosted the ball. It benefited Feeding America, which supplies food to low-income Americans.

In the Headlines

Rihanna was scheduled to perform at the Grammy Awards on February 8, 2009. She was nominated for three awards, too. But she had to cancel. Her boyfriend, 19-year-old Chris Brown, was arrested for **allegedly** attacking her after the couple argued the night before. After the incident, parents and teachers reminded children that relationships should never involve physical or emotional abuse. As fans expressed concern, Rihanna released a statement saying she "is doing well and deeply appreciates the outpouring of support at this difficult time."

Staying Strong

As she thought about her future, Rihanna traveled to Barbados to be with her family. In the spring of 2009, she began to write new songs and work on her next album. "She's someone … who has something to say," Rihanna's producer, Ryan Tedder, told *People*. "She's confident and strong."

Meanwhile, fans enjoyed Rihanna's most recent release, *Good Girl Gone Bad: The Remixes.* The album, released in January 2009, features new versions of songs from Rihanna's third album.

Rihanna's Favorites

- ✔ **Foods:** West Indian and Italian
- ✔ **Singers:** Mariah Carey, Alicia Keys, Beyoncé Knowles
- ✔ **Color:** Green
- ✔ **Snack:** Cheetos
- ✔ **Movie:** *Borat*
- ✔ **Video Game:** *Guitar Hero* for Xbox
- ✔ **Candy:** Snickers bars

By The Numbers

2 Number of minutes Jay-Z says it took him to see that Rihanna was a star

Less than 8 Number of months between the release of Rihanna's first and second albums

16 Age Rihanna was when she moved to the United States

More than 100,000 Number of people who attended Rihanna's July 2008 concert in Casablanca, Morocco

115,000 Number of copies Rihanna's second album, *A Girl Like Me*, sold during its first week

11 million Approximate number of records Rihanna has sold worldwide through 2008

Big Plans

What's next for Rihanna? She'd like to do more songwriting and acting in movies, as well as design her own clothing line. By the time she is 30, she told *InStyle*, "I want to have already started my family and have some businesses of my own. A fashion line, a makeup line, and I still want to be doing what I'm doing at a much bigger **capacity**."

▼ Rihanna performs at a Super Bowl party in early 2009.

Time Line

1988 Robyn Rihanna Fenty is born on February 20 in St. Michael, Barbados.

2003 Rihanna auditions for music producer Evan Rogers in Barbados.

2004 Rihanna moves from Barbados to Connecticut to live with Rogers and his wife as she works on her demo.

2005 Rihanna is signed by rapper Jay-Z, then head of Def Jam Recordings. She releases her debut album, *Music of the Sun*, which sells 69,000 copies in its first week.

 **2006** Rihanna releases her second album, *A Girl Like Me*, which sells more than 115,000 copies in its first week.

 **2007** Rihanna releases a new album called *Good Girl Gone Bad*, which goes to number two on the Billboard 200 chart. She goes on her first headlining world tour.

2008 Rihanna releases *Good Girl Gone Bad: Reloaded.* She wins her first Grammy Award.

2009 Rihanna releases *Good Girl Gone Bad: The Remixes.*

Glossary

addiction: the condition of being dependent on something that is habit forming, especially alcohol or drugs

ambassador: an official representative of a country or group

auditioned: did a trial performance

ballads: slow, romantic songs

capacity: a person's ability to do something

chorus: the part of a song that recurs after each verse

collaboration: the act of working together

cover versions: recordings or performances of a song previously recorded by someone else

debut: the first public appearance

demo: a recording made to present a song to a record producer

duet: a song for two performers

inauguration: the ceremonial installation into public office, such as when a president takes office

producer: someone who is in charge of making a record, film, or TV show

reggae: a type of music developed in Jamaica that blends many styles, including jazz and rhythm and blues

remixes: songs that are mixed in a new way and rerecorded

tribute: a compliment or honor

To Find Out More

Books

Arenofsky, Janice. *Beyoncé Knowles: A Biography*. New York: Greenwood Press, 2009.

Krumenauer, Heidi. *Rihanna* (Blue Banner Biography). Hockessin, DE: Mitchell Lane Publishers, 2009.

Orr, Tamra. *Barbados* (The Caribbean Today). Broomall, PA: Mason Crest Publishers, 2009.

Web Sites

Believe Foundation
www.believerihanna.com
This site for Rihanna's foundation includes photos and information on how you can help.

National Teen Dating Abuse Helpline
www.loveisrespect.org
This site for teens and parents provides information about teen dating abuse and how to develop healthy relationships.

Rihanna
www.rihannanow.com
Check out Rihanna's official web site, featuring news, tour dates, photos, and videos.

Major Awards

American Music Awards
2007 Favorite Female Artist (Soul/R&B)
2008 Favorite Female Artist (Soul/R&B); Favorite Female
Artist (Pop/Rock)

Billboard Music Awards
2006 Female Artist of the Year; Pop 100 Artist of the Year;
Female Hot 100 Artist of the Year

Grammy Awards
2008 Best Rap/Sung Collaboration for
"Umbrella"

MTV Video Music Awards
2008 Monster Single of the Year and
Video of the Year for "Umbrella"

Teen Choice Awards
2006 Female Breakout Artist; Choice
Female R&B Artist
2007 Choice Music, R&B Artist

Source Notes

p. 5 Sia Tiambi Barnes, "The Scoop: Diddy, Rihanna, Rakim," BET.com, February 25, 2008, www.bet.com/Music/News/musicnews_thescoop_2.25.htm?Referrer=%7B8952391D-B74E-4B69-87D9-C7F68BFF0A06%7D.

p. 7 George Epaminondas, "Rihanna, Revealed," *InStyle*, August 2008, 196.

p. 8 Christian Hoard, "Island Girl," *Rolling Stone*, September 8, 2005.

p. 9 Carissa Rosenberg, "Rihanna: Style Star," *Seventeen*, December 2007, 64.

p. 11 Epaminondas, 196.

p. 12 Brooke Hauser, "Bright Young Thing," *Allure*, January 2008, 146.

p. 13 (top) Hauser, 146.

p. 13 (center) Hauser, 146.

p. 13 (bottom) Rosenberg, 64.

p. 14 Margeaux Watson, "Caribbean Queen: Rihanna," *Entertainment Weekly*, June 29, 2007, www.ew.com/ew/article/0,,20043393,00.html.

p. 17 Watson, www.ew.com/ew/article/0,,20043393,00.html.

p. 19 "Rihanna Interview," KidzWorld, www.kidzworld.com/article/5853-rihanna-interview.

p. 20 "Rihanna Interview."

p. 21 Tiffany McGee, "Sounds Off: Rihanna," *People*, August 29, 2005, 49.

p. 23 Melody K. Hoffman, "Rihanna Loses 'Good Girl' Image With New Look, New Sound," *Jet*, June 11, 2007, 54.

p. 24 Hauser, 146.

p. 26 Stephen M. Silverman, "Mary J. Blige Dominates Billboard Awards," *People*, December 5, 2006, http://www.people.com/people/article/0,,1565993,00.html.

p. 27 Hoffman, 55.

p. 29 Candice Rainey, "Good Girl Gone Great," *Elle*, May 4, 2008, www.elle.com/Entertainment/Cover-Shoots/Rihanna-Elle-Magazine-June-2008.

p. 30 Jayson Rodriguez, "Rihanna's 'Umbrella' Was 'The Perfect Storm' That Almost Didn't Happen: Behind the Grammys," MTV, February 6, 2008, www.mtv.com/news/articles/1580820/20080201/rihanna.jhtml.

p. 31 Hauser, 146.

p. 33 "Rihanna: Biography," *People*, www.people.com/people/rihanna/biography.

p. 37 Mike Fleeman and Tiffany McGee, "Rihanna Assures Fans She 'Remains Strong,' " People.com, February 20, 2009. www.people.com/people/article/0,,20260474,00.html.

p. 38 Eunice Oh, "Producer: Rihanna is Confident and Strong," People.com, April 24, 2009. http://www.people.com/people/article/0,,20274525,00.html.

p. 39 Epaminondas, 196.

True or False Answers

Page 6 True.

Page 8 False. She really doesn't like vegetables! But she stays healthy by eating lots of fruit and drinking water.

Page 12 False. Barbados is in the Caribbean, which is in the Atlantic Ocean.

Page 19 False. Early in her career, Rihanna opened for pop star Gwen Stefani.

Page 20 False. It reached number two.

Page 24 True.

Page 36 True.

Page 38 False. She was nominated for three Grammy Awards but did not win any.

Rihanna was the opening act for singer Gwen Stefani.

Barbados lies in the Atlantic Ocean.

Index

About the Author

Mary Kate Frank is a writer and editor. Her work has appeared in newspapers and magazines including the *New York Times*, the *Star-Ledger of Newark, NJ*, *Health*, *Teen Newsweek*, and *Quick & Simple*, as well as in the anthology *Twentysomething Essays by Twentysomething Writers* (Random House, 2006). She holds a master's degree in journalism from New York University and lives in New York City.